LIVING THINGS

ROBERT SNEDDEN

Flowers

A⁺
Smart Apple Media

Published by Smart Apple Media
2140 Howard Drive West
North Mankato, MN 56003

Designed by Guy Callaby
Edited by Pip Morgan
Illustrations by Guy Callaby
Picture research by Su Alexander

Picture acknowledgements
Title page Aflo/Nature Picture Library; 3 George D. Lepp/Corbis;
4 Richard Cummins/Corbis; 5 Paul A.Souders/Corbis; 6 Bernard
Castelein/Nature Picture Library; 7t Jean E. Roche/Nature Picture Library,
b Phil Schermeister/Corbis; 9t Guy Callaby, b Roger Tidman/Corbis;
10 Visuals Unlimited/Corbis; 11t Geoff Simpson/Nature Picture Library,
b Galen Rowell/Corbis; 13 John Dransfield; 14 George D. Lepp/Corbis;
15t Lester Lefkowitz/Corbis, b Neil Lucas/Nature Picture Library; 16 Bob
Krist/Corbis; 17t Lester V.Bergman/Corbis, b Kennan Ward/Corbis;
18 Anup Shah/Nature Picture Library; 19t Tony Wharton; Frank Lane
Picture Agency/Corbis, b Science Source/Science Photo Library;
21t Duncan McEwan/Nature Picture Library, b Aflo/Nature Picture
Library; 22 Guenter Rossenbach/Zefa/Corbis; 23 Geoff Simpson/
Nature Picture Library; 24t DK Limited/Corbis, b Kenneth R. Robertson;
25t Tom Mangelsen/Nature Picture Library, b Guy Callaby;
27 Photowood Inc/Corbis; 28 Jeff Foott/Nature Picture Library;
29 Kazuyoshi Nomachi/Corbis.

Front cover: William Manning/Corbis

Printed in China

Library of Congress Cataloging-in-Publication Data

Snedden, Robert.
Flowers / by Robert Snedden.
p. cm. — (Living things)
Includes index.
ISBN-13: 978-1-59920-078-1
1. Flowers—Juvenile literature. I. Title.

QK49.S67 2007
582.13—dc22   2006039608

First Edition

9 8 7 6 5 4 3 2 1

Contents

4   What is a flower?

6   Plants without flowers

8   Underground anchors

10   Support above the ground

12   Leaves

14   Food for free

16   Specialized leaves

18   Plant defenses

20   Flowers

22   A new generation

24   Seeds and fruits

26   Time to grow

28   Floral planet

30   Glossary

32   Index

What is a flower?

When you think of flowers, what comes to mind? Do you think of the brightly colored and pleasant-smelling plants that cheer up our parks and gardens in the spring and summer? Do you think of flowers in bunches to give as a gift?

The variety of flowering plants

There are around 250,000 different kinds of flowering plants in the world. The enormous variety includes potatoes, oak trees, parsley— even grass. Flowering plants range in size from tiny duckweeds that float on streams and ponds to eucalyptus trees that grow to heights of almost 300 feet (91 m).

Flowers aren't just nice to have around. Without them we would starve. All our fruits and vegetables, rice and beans, and all the grains we eat, such as oats, barley, and wheat, come from flowering plants.

BELOW *A carpet of bluebonnets is an unmistakable sign that spring has arrived in Texas.*

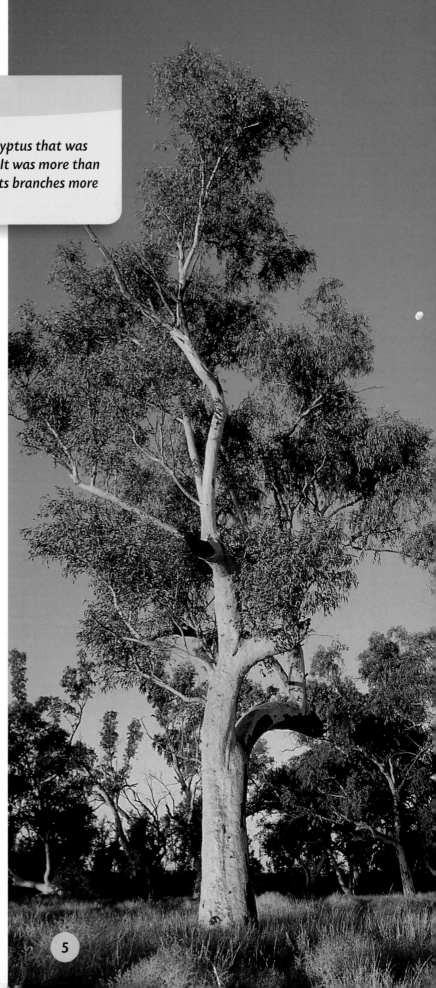

WOW!

The tallest tree ever recorded was a eucalyptus that was cut down in Victoria, Australia, in 1885. It was more than 374 feet (114 m) tall, with the lowest of its branches more than 246 feet (75 m) above the ground.

Parts of a plant

Often when people think of a bunch of flowers, they don't give much thought to the rest of the plant. But a flower is just one part of a flowering plant. In addition to its flowers, a flowering plant also has leaves, roots, and a stem, and each part is as important as the other. In this book, we will look at all the parts of a flowering plant—not just its flowers.

The enormous variety of flowering plants, from rare and exotic orchids to the widespread dandelion, have certain things in common because they all perform the same tasks. Let's discover just what a plant has to do to live and grow.

RIGHT *Australia's eucalyptus trees are the world's tallest flowering plants.*

WOW!

The world's smallest flowering plants are duckweeds called Wolffia. The whole plant is less than 0.03 inches (1 mm) long. You could easily fit one inside this letter "o."

Plants without flowers

In this book, we are looking at a particular kind of plant—flowering plants—but not all plants have flowers. Here is a brief look at plants that don't have flowers.

Mosses

Mosses are small plants that grow close to the ground in damp and shady places. They often grow together in large numbers that form mats or clumps on a forest floor. They do not have roots but are anchored to the ground by thin tubes. They don't have stems either. Mosses reproduce by producing tiny spores that grow into new plants. There are around 19,000 different types of mosses and similar plants, such as liverworts and hornworts.

ABOVE Mosses, like this hair moss, don't have flowers. They produce spores from long stalks.

Ferns

Ferns have roots, stems, and a number of long, thin leaves, called fronds, growing from either side of the stem. They do not produce flowers but form spores on the undersides of their fronds. Ferns need moist conditions to survive and almost all the world's ferns—there are about 12,000 types—grow in tropical forests. Some can grow as much as 82 feet (25 m) tall.

RIGHT *Tree ferns stand tall in the rain forest on the island of Réunion in the Indian Ocean.*

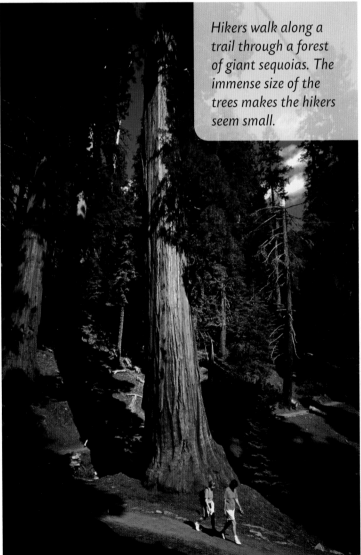

Hikers walk along a trail through a forest of giant sequoias. The immense size of the trees makes the hikers seem small.

Naked seeds

Plants called gymnosperms produce seeds but don't have flowers. The name gymnosperm means "naked seed," their seeds are not protected by fruits, as those of flowering plants are. Most gymnosperms are shrubs or trees.

The most common gymnosperms are conifers, or evergreen trees, such as pine, spruce, and cedar. Most conifers have needle-like leaves, which are an adaptation to the cold conditions of the northern forests where many conifers live. The gymnosperms also include giant redwood trees and sequoias, which are the largest plants on the planet. There are about 750 different types of gymnosperms.

WOW!

The most massive living thing in the world is a giant sequoia tree called General Sherman, which grows in California. It is more than 272 feet (83 m) tall and may weigh about 2,000 (1,814 t) tons. The biggest animal, the blue whale, weighs around 125 tons (113 t).

Underground anchors

Some of the most important parts of a flowering plant are usually hidden from sight. Yet they may be the biggest part of the plant, holding it firmly in place. These are the plant's roots.

Essential roots

Keeping a plant anchored to the ground is important, but roots also perform another essential job. When a seed sprouts, the root is the first thing to appear. The plant sends out its roots through the ground, searching for the water and minerals it needs to grow.

FIBROUS ROOT SYSTEM

A fibrous root system has a number of roots of similar size that branch out through the soil.

TAPROOT SYSTEM

A taproot system has one main root that pushes down into the soil. Smaller roots branch out from it.

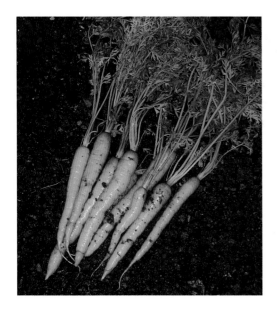

ABOVE *Carrots have a taproot system. Food stored in the roots provide us with a tasty vegetable.*

Main roots and branching roots

Some types of plants have one main root that goes deep into the soil. This is called a taproot. Smaller branch roots grow out from the taproot. The taproot is often used as a food supply by the plant. Some vegetables we eat, such as beetroots, are actually taproots.

Other plants have a large number of small roots that spread out through the soil. These are called fibrous roots. Grasses have fibrous root systems. Plants with fibrous roots are more difficult to pull up.

Root hairs

Roots grow from their tips. The growing tip of a root is protected by a dome-shaped root cap that pushes forward into the soil. Just behind the tip there are root hairs that extend out and cling tightly to the soil particles. A plant might have billions of root hairs, which greatly increase the surface area through which it absorbs water and minerals. As the root pushes through the soil, the root hairs are continually rubbed off and replaced. Some plants grow 100 million new root hairs every day.

Inside the roots there are tubes that carry water and minerals up from the roots to the rest of the plant. Other tubes bring food down from the leaves for storage and to provide the roots with the energy they need to grow. The water-carrying tubes are called xylem, and the food-carrying tubes are called phloem.

RIGHT *Erosion of the soil has exposed the spreading roots of these pine trees. Ninety percent of a pine tree's roots are in the top 1.6 feet (0.5 m) of soil.*

WOW!

The deepest roots are those of plants growing in dry regions—they may have to go down a long way to find water. The roots of a wild fig tree in South Africa go down 394 feet (120 m) into the ground.

Support above the ground

Almost all flowering plants have stems that usually grow upright and provide support above the ground for a plant's buds, leaves, flowers, and fruits.

Main pipeline

Stems vary in size and appearance, from the stubby stem of a cabbage to the tall trunk of a tree. The stem is the main pipeline in the plant's transportation system, carrying water, minerals, and food (in the form of sugars) to the various parts of the plant. It is like the plant's main artery.

Creeping stems

The stems of some plants, such as strawberries, creep along the ground. These stems are called runners. The stems of some other plants, such as irises, grow under the ground. These are called rhizomes, and they send up new shoots and leaves to grow above ground.

LEFT *In this cross section of a plant stem, you can clearly see the network of tubes that carry water and nutrients to all parts of the plant.*

Growing buds

A plant stem produces buds from which new shoots, leaves, and flowers grow. Buds first appear at the tip of the growing stem, and they later appear where older leaves are attached to the stem. As it grows, the bud may be protected by bud scales, which are a special type of leaf. As the new leaves develop, the stem holds them in the best position to catch the most sunlight.

LEFT *A new leaf opens out from its bud on this European beech tree.*

RIGHT *Bamboo plants grow from underground rhizomes that send up new shoots.*

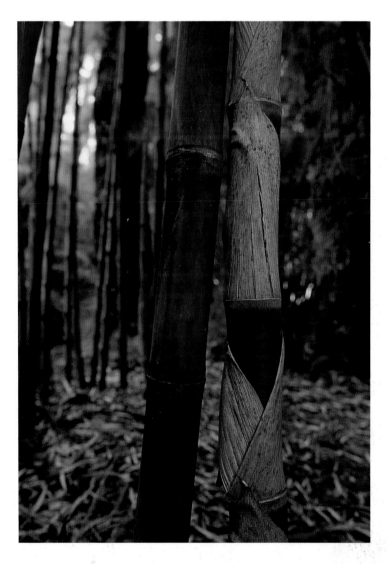

Waterproofing

All stems have a waterproof coating so that the water moving up from the roots isn't lost. Most plants have a thin, waxy coating, while woody plants, such as trees and shrubs, have a bark covering that protects the stem. Some plants grow spines or thorns on their stems to discourage animals from eating them.

Stem stores

Cacti and other plants that grow in dry places use their stems as water stores. Other plants use their stems to store food. Bulbs, such as onions, are actually short stems surrounded by fleshy leaves. Tubers, such as potatoes, are another form of underground stem storage. The "eyes" on a potato are actually the beginnings of buds that will form new leaves.

Leaves

All of a plant's leaves together make up its foliage. Leaves come in many different shapes and sizes, depending on the type of plant and the conditions it grows in.

Needle-shaped

Triangle-shaped

LEAF SHAPES

A typical plant leaf is broad and oval-shaped. There are many variations in the size and shape of leaves, as you can see from the selection on these pages.

The parts of a leaf

The leaves of most flowering plants have two main parts. Most leaves have a short stalk that holds the leaf out from the stem. This is the leafstalk, or petiole. Not all flowering plants have petioles. Grasses, for example, do not have them. Some flowering plants have very large petioles. If you munch a stalk of celery, you're actually eating a petiole.

The flat part of the leaf is called the blade. Often you can see a network of veins running through the blade. These are part of the plant's transportation system, carrying food and water back and forth between the leaves and the roots. These veins are tough and strong and also help prevent the leaf from collapsing or tearing.

Leaf shapes

Leaves come in a great variety of shapes. They may be simple leaves, with just one blade on the leafstalk, or compound leaves, with two or more blades. A leaf can be narrow and sword-shaped, like a blade of grass, or big and round, like the floating leaf of a water lily. Many leaves are simply oval in shape, but there are also many with complex shapes.

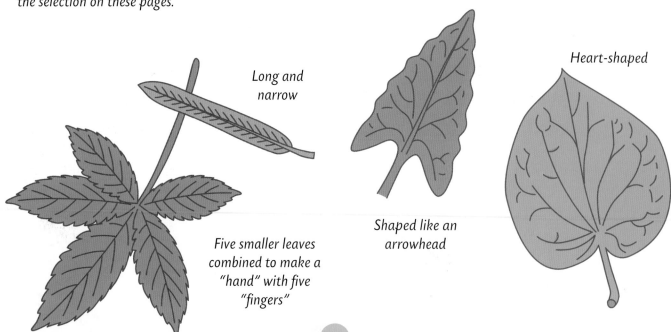

Long and narrow

Heart-shaped

Shaped like an arrowhead

Five smaller leaves combined to make a "hand" with five "fingers"

WOW!

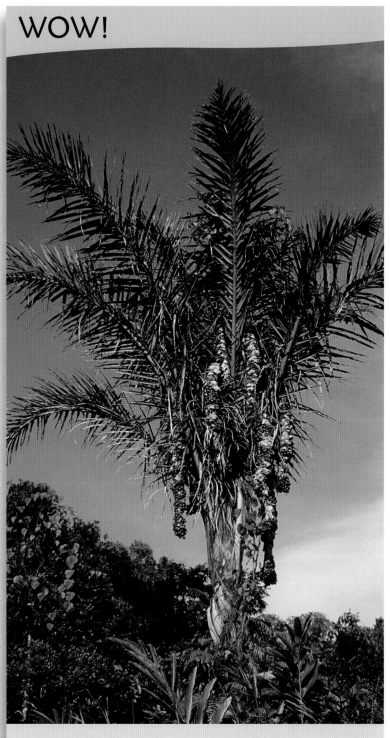

The world's biggest leaves grow on palm trees. The massive leaves of the African raffia palm are 79 feet (24 m) long. In contrast, pygmy weed, which is found in California, has leaves that are just over 0.03 inches (1 mm) across.

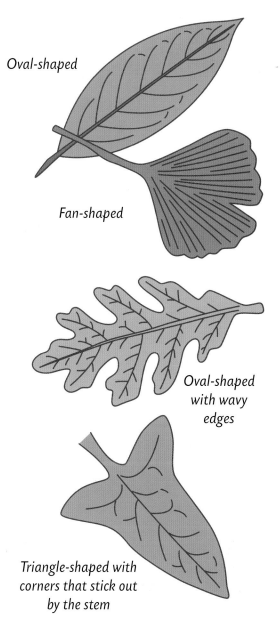

Oval-shaped

Fan-shaped

Oval-shaped with wavy edges

Triangle-shaped with corners that stick out by the stem

A leaf's surface

Like the stem, the plant's leaves are covered in a waxy waterproof coating called a cuticle. However, the leaves can't be entirely sealed with this coating because, like other living things, plants need air. There are many tiny openings, or pores, in a leaf's surface. The plant can open these pores to let air in and close them to save water.

Food for free

A plant's leaves are its food factories. Making food is the most important job the leaves do. They gather energy from sunlight and use it to make sugar. This process is called photosynthesis.

First link in the chain

All living things have certain things in common and one of these is that they all need energy. Animals get their energy from the food they eat. Plants, on the other hand, can make their own food. They capture the energy of sunlight and store it in their leaves, stalks, fruits, and roots.

This energy is then available first to animals that eat the plants, and then to animals that eat the plant-eaters. This is a food chain. In almost all cases the first link in a food chain is a plant.

BELOW *This lush rain forest on the Caribbean island of Grenada is only a tiny fraction of the staggering amount of plant growth on the earth.*

Making glucose

Plants use sunlight energy, carbon dioxide gas from the air, and water from the soil to make glucose, a type of sugar. This process is called photosynthesis, which means "making from light." You may have come across glucose in some candies and drinks. Glucose gives plants the energy they need. It can be turned into different kinds of sugar and starches for storage and combined with minerals from the soil for plant growth.

RIGHT *This magnified section of a plant leaf shows the tiny green chloroplasts inside the cells.*

It's good to be green

Photosynthesis takes place inside the cells of a leaf in tiny bodies called chloroplasts, which are too small to see without a microscope. They contain a chemical called chlorophyll, which only plants have. Chlorophyll gives plants their green color and is used in photosynthesis to capture the energy of sunlight.

In addition to making food for the plant, photosynthesis also produces oxygen. Practically every living thing needs oxygen to stay alive, so this is another vital role plants play in the living world. Without plants and photosynthesis there would be no life as we know it.

LEFT *Plants are a source of food for the world's animals, such as this African lowland gorilla in Zaire.*

WOW!

Photosynthesis produces 240 billion tons (218 billion t) of new plant material every year across the world. In a year, 10 square feet (1 sq m) of rain forest produces the energy equivalent of 5.5 pounds (2.5 kg) of sugar.

Specialized leaves

Leaves aren't just food factories. They can be the plant's toolbox, carrying out many important tasks, including support and protection.

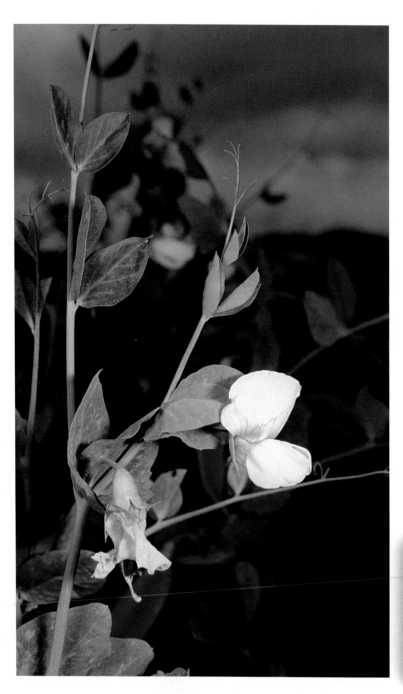

Winding tendrils

Some of the leaves of climbing plants are threadlike and coiling. These tendrils circle slowly in the air until they find something to cling to, and then they wind themselves around it. This gives the plant support as it climbs upward. Peas, grape vines, and ivy all produce tendrils.

Swollen leaves

Succulents are plants that live in dry places, and their thick, swollen leaves are adapted to store water. The leaves are either hairy or waxy to help reduce water loss. Succulents include house leeks, stonecrops, and odd-looking plants called living stones.

LEFT *The snow pea plant grows tendrils that wind around things, such as a fence or the branching stem of another plant.*

WOW!

The world's biggest cactus is the giant saguaro, which can grow up to 66 feet (20 m) tall. It can store around six tons (5.4 t) of water in its stem.

Cactus spines

At first glance, a cactus might not appear to have any leaves, but in fact it does. Its leaves have become clusters of spines dotted around its thick stem. Cacti are a type of succulent, storing water in their stems rather than their leaves.

Cactus leaves serve a double purpose. Cacti grow in hot, dry places and having leaves that are greatly reduced in size helps cut down on water loss. The sharp spines also give the cactus some protection from desert animals that try to eat it.

Drip-tips and water wings

Plants that live in damp conditions also have special leaf adaptations. The weight of too much rainwater might be enough to break the branches of a tree. Rainforest trees have leaves with pointed tips that turn downward. These "drip-tips" make it easy for rainwater to run off the leaves.

The big floating leaves of water lilies are filled with air spaces. The air trapped inside acts like water wings, keeping the leaf afloat on the surface of the pond. A water-repellent, waxy substance covers the top of the leaf. This helps prevent the leaf from sinking under the weight of the water collecting on it.

ABOVE *Needle-like leaves protect this cactus from hungry animals and also help prevent water loss.*

Insect eaters

Some plants that live in poor soil add to their diet by capturing insects. The Venus flytrap has leaves that are hinged down the middle. If an insect lands on the leaf, the two halves snap shut, trapping it inside. Curved spines around the outside of the leaf stop the doomed insect from escaping.

LEFT *The two halves of a leaf on this Venus flytrap are about to snap shut around an ant, which the plant will later digest as food.*

Plant defenses

Plants can't pull up their roots and escape if something starts to eat them. But some plants have a few defenses to rely on—some are obvious and others not so obvious.

ABOVE *The grasslands of Africa are eaten by countless grazing animals, such as these wildebeests in Kenya, but the grasses will grow back.*

Keep growing

Unlike animals, plants can lose large parts of themselves and still keep growing. Grasses, for example, grow from the base of their leaves, down near the soil, and not from the tip. So no matter how much an animal nibbles away at the grass, as long as some green part remains, the grass will grow back again.

Thorns, spines, and prickles

Like the spiny leaves of the cactus, other plants are also armed for survival. While spines are specialized leaves, thorns are specialized short stems that end in a sharp point. The hawthorn is an example of a plant that is well equipped with thorns. Although we often talk about roses having thorns, they actually have prickles. The difference is that a prickle is attached to the surface of the stem and breaks off easily.

ABOVE *The stem of a dog rose has sharp prickles which keep animals from eating it.*

ABOVE *Plants that are attacked by insects may release chemicals that attract predators such as this soldier bug, which then kill the plant eaters.*

Chemical defenses

Many plants have less obvious, but just as effective, ways of defending themselves—they use chemical weapons. The variety of these defenses is astonishing. Some plants produce chemicals that repel insects and other animals, discouraging them from feeding or laying their eggs. Others produce poison that kills a feeding insect.

Some plants produce chemicals that interfere with an insect's development, so it doesn't develop as it should. Other plant chemicals can stop an insect's digestive system from working properly, so it starves. Some plants can mimic insect alarm scents, so they flee as if there was an insect-eating predator present. There is nonstop chemical warfare in the plant world!

WOW!

One of the most poisonous substances in the natural world is a chemical called ricin. It is produced in the seeds of the castor bean plant. If an adult human ate only 0.00004 ounces (0.001 g) of ricin, it would be fatal.

Flowers

What makes flowering plants different from other plants is their flowers. There are a huge variety of flower shapes, scents, and colors. They can be a single flower or in huge clusters. So what exactly is a flower?

A new generation

A flower is a flowering plant's reproductive organ. Its purpose is to make sure that the plant can produce seeds that eventually grow into new plants.

FLOWER STRUCTURE

The four parts of a flower are the sepals, petals, stamens, and carpels. Each stamen has a filament and an anther. Each carpel has a stigma, style, and ovary.

Parts of a flower

Flowers develop from buds growing along the plant stem. A flower is really a collection of specialized leaves.

Most types of flowers have four main parts: sepals, petals, stamens, and carpels. The sepals are the green parts on the outside of the flower. They protect the flower bud and sometimes drop off after it opens. The petals are usually the most colorful parts of a flower. Inside the petals are the stamens and the carpels.

The stamens are the male parts of a flower; each stamen has a long, narrow stalk called a filament, on the end of which is an anther. The anther produces the flower's pollen, which looks like fine dust. The carpels are the female parts of the flower. Each carpel has a stigma at the top, a stalk called a style, and an ovary at the bottom that produces the ovules that will eventually form seeds.

The flowers of some types of plants contain both male and female parts. Other types grow separate male and female flowers on the same individual plant. There are also types in which there are male flowers on one plant and female flowers on another.

Florets and colorful leaves

Some flowers that look like single flowers, such as daisies, dandelions, and sunflowers, are not single at all. They are made up of a tightly packed mass of very tiny flowers, called florets. What look like petals are colorful leaves called bracts that form a cup around the cluster of florets. Some flowering plants, such as poinsettias, have bracts that are more brightly colored than the flowers.

ABOVE *Long male catkins and smaller red female flowers grow beside each other on this common alder tree.*

ABOVE *This sunflower is not a single flower at all, but is made of many small florets packed closely together.*

WOW!

The biggest flower in the world is the stinking corpse lily, a parasite that grows in the tropical forests of Southeast Asia. It is nearly 3.3 feet (1 m) across, and as you might guess from the name, it doesn't smell very nice!

A new generation

Before a flower can produce seeds, pollen from male anthers has to reach its female stigma. This process is called pollination, and it involves one of nature's most important partnerships.

Some plants can pollinate their own flowers. Pollen from a flower reaches the ovary on the same flower or an ovary in another flower on the same plant. This is called self-pollination. Other types of flowers need pollen from another plant of the same kind. This is called cross-pollination and is done by a pollinator, such as the wind or an animal.

This beach grass on a sand dune in Germany is pollinated by the wind.

On the wind

Flowers that need the wind to carry their pollen long distances have long anthers and produce masses of lightweight pollen. Wind-pollinated flowers are often small and may have tiny petals or no petals at all. Grasses and many types of trees are wind-pollinated.

Flowers and animals

Flower petals are often brightly colored. They may also produce fragrant oils that give the flower a pleasing smell. This display of sights and smells attracts animal pollinators.

Most animal pollinators are insects, although birds and bats may also be pollinators. Flowers and insects work well together. The flower needs to be pollinated, and the insect needs food. The flower produces a sweet, sugary, energy-giving liquid called nectar, which the insect drinks.

To reach the nectar, an insect brushes against the flower's stamens and collects pollen grains on its hairy body. When the insect visits another flower, the insect touches the stigma and leaves some pollen grains behind. When this happens, the flower is pollinated.

pollen grain

sperm cells

pollen tube

egg

ovary

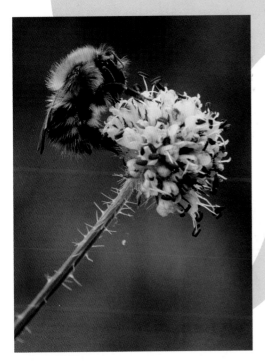

LEFT *When an insect such as this bumblebee visits a flower, it feeds on the nectar and collects pollen on its body.*

Setting seed

Now the flower can produce seeds. When the pollen grain reaches the stigma, it begins to grow a very fine tube. This passes down through the style until it reaches the ovule inside the ovary. Tiny sperm cells move down the tube to fertilize the ovule. Now it can become a seed.

WOW!

A corn pollen tube might have to grow over seven inches (20 cm) to reach the ovule and complete fertilization.

POLLEN TUBE

A pollen grain releases two sperm cells, which move downward through a pollen tube to the ovary. One will fertilize an egg to form a new plant embryo; the other will form the embryo's food source.

Seeds and fruits

Seeds come in a large assortment of shapes and sizes. They may be so small and light that they float in the air or so big that they weigh several pounds. Inside all of them are the beginnings of a new plant.

Seed parts

Inside the seed of every flowering plant there is an embryo, formed when the sperm cells from the pollen grain fertilized the ovule. The embryo is usually surrounded by a store of food made of energy-rich starch and other substances. All this is enclosed within a protective seed coat.

Many flowering plant embryos also have either one or two seed leaves as food stores. These can take up most of the space inside the seed. Grasses, orchids, and palm trees all have one seed leaf, while oak trees, beans, and sunflowers have two seed leaves.

LEFT *The wings of this maple seed keep it in the air longer so it can land farther from the parent tree.*

Fruit formation

After the seeds are produced, the flower's carpels turn into fruits. Only flowering plants have fruits; no other type of plant does. When you think of fruit, apples, oranges, and pears might come to mind. But the pod of a pea is also a fruit, and so are a cucumber and the fluff that blows off a dandelion head.

LEFT *The seeds of an orchid are so tiny and light that they can be carried on the wind.*

Spreading seeds

Fruits have two jobs. One is to protect the seeds, and the other is to make sure the seeds are spread as widely as possible. Spreading seeds is called dispersal.

The fruits of the sycamore tree spin like tiny propeller blades as they fall. This helps them stay in the air longer, so they travel farther from the tree. Feathery dandelion fluff is also carried by the wind. Some fruits burst as they dry out, spraying seeds in all directions.

Animals carry many seeds and fruits. Some fruits, such the burdock, have hooks that stick to an animal's fur as it brushes past the plant. Other plants have colorful fruits that are good to eat. The animal eats the fruit but does not digest the seeds inside and they pass out of the animal in its droppings. The droppings may even provide a natural fertilizer for the seed to grow!

ABOVE *These waxwings are feasting on berries and will leave the seeds in their droppings.*

WOW!

The world's biggest seeds belong to the coco de mer, a palm tree on the Seychelles Islands in the Indian Ocean. These "coconuts" of the sea can be nearly 3.5 feet (1 m) around and weigh 40 pounds (18 kg) or more. The smallest seeds are orchid seeds—one million of these would weigh less than 0.04 ounces (1 g).

Time to grow

Most seeds go through a quiet phase of inactivity, or dormancy, when not much seems to be happening. When conditions are right, the embryo inside will start to grow. This is germination.

Springing to life

Seeds do not usually begin growing right away. They need the right temperature and the right amount of moisture. In places where winters are cold, the seeds may wait for the warmth of spring before germinating. Most seeds grow best at temperatures between 64°F (18°C) and 84°F (29°C). In dry areas, seeds do not germinate until it rains. Moisture is important because it softens the seed coat, so the embryo growing inside can break through.

Primary roots

The first thing to emerge from the seed is the primary root, or radicle. The radicle is important because the one thing that isn't stored in the seed is water. It pushes down into the soil to begin drawing up water and minerals to feed the germinating seed. Once the root is established, the shoot begins to grow.

STAGES OF GERMINATION

The first stages in the growth of a new plant change a seed into a seedling.

seed leaves

radicle

seed

From seed to seedling

The shoot that pushes up toward the light must not be damaged. Many plant shoots have stems which bend to form a loop so that the side of the stem comes up through the soil first. This helps protect the delicate bud at the tip of the shoot.

The seed leaves of some plants stay beneath the ground, providing food for the growing shoot. Other kinds of plants have seed leaves which appear aboveground first. They usually look different from the leaves the plant will grow later. As the new seedling's leaves begin to grow, they provide it with food by photosynthesis. The seedling no longer needs the food stored in the seed leaves and they wither away. The seed has become a new, young plant.

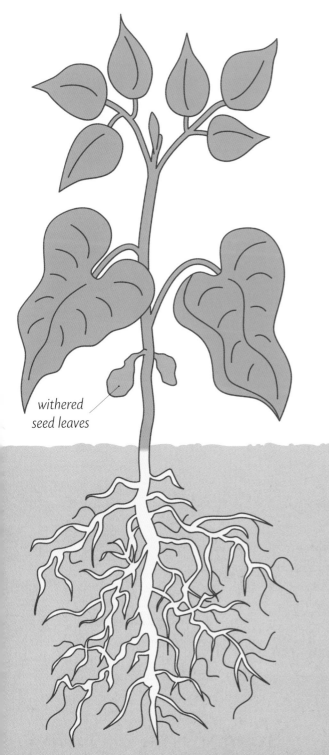

withered
seed leaves

WOW!

Some seeds can stay dormant longer than others before they germinate. The seeds of some maples die unless they germinate within two weeks. In contrast, 2,000-year-old seeds from lotus plants have successfully germinated.

Floral planet

It is difficult to imagine what the world would be like without flowers. It would certainly be a much less colorful place. It would be a much quieter place, too, because the animals would starve with nothing to eat.

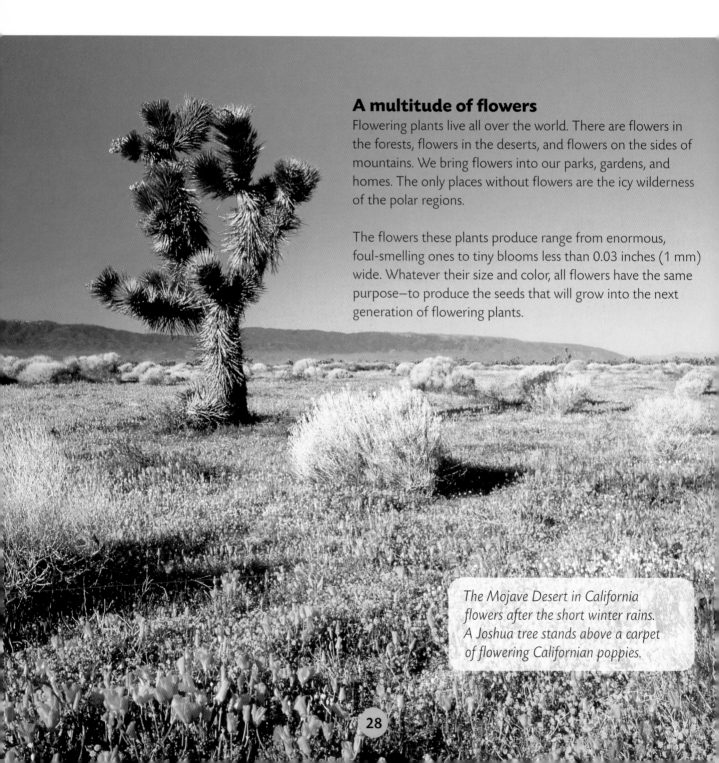

A multitude of flowers

Flowering plants live all over the world. There are flowers in the forests, flowers in the deserts, and flowers on the sides of mountains. We bring flowers into our parks, gardens, and homes. The only places without flowers are the icy wilderness of the polar regions.

The flowers these plants produce range from enormous, foul-smelling ones to tiny blooms less than 0.03 inches (1 mm) wide. Whatever their size and color, all flowers have the same purpose—to produce the seeds that will grow into the next generation of flowering plants.

The Mojave Desert in California flowers after the short winter rains. A Joshua tree stands above a carpet of flowering Californian poppies.

BELOW *When logging companies cut down trees and clear the forests, they threaten not only plants but also the animals that depend on the plants for food and shelter.*

Primary producers

There are more flowering plants than all the other types of plants put together. Their role in the living world is vital. Because flowering plants make their own food through photosynthesis, they are sometimes called primary producers. Plants are the basis of almost every food chain. They make the energy that other living things depend on. If an animal doesn't eat plants, it eats another animal that does eat plants. During photosynthesis, plants also produce oxygen, without which we could not survive.

Plants and humans

We rely on flowering plants for many things. Four-fifths of the food eaten by the world's human population—all the cereal, fruits, and vegetables—comes from flowering plants. We use wood from trees for fuel and for building and we use fibers from plants, such as cotton, to make clothes. Flowering plants are also a source of many medicines.

Pollution and the loss of habitats threaten the welfare of plants just as much as they affect other living things. If a plant becomes extinct, so do the animals that feed on that plant, and the animals that feed on them. If the first link of a food chain is gone, all other living things in the chain will be threatened.

Glossary

Adaptation A feature of a living thing that makes it better suited to its lifestyle.

Anther The part of a flower where male pollen is produced.

Bud An undeveloped shoot or flower that has not yet opened.

Carpel The female part of a flower that is made up of the stigma, style, and ovary.

Chlorophyll A chemical that captures sunlight energy for use in photosynthesis and gives plants their green color.

Conifer A type of evergreen tree that produces seeds in cones rather than flowers.

Cuticle A waxy, protective layer on the outside of a leaf.

Embryo The young plant inside a seed.

Fertilize To make an ovule fertile; sperm cells in pollen grains fertilize an ovule so that a seed can grow.

Florets Tiny flowers that make up the flower heads of plants such as sunflowers.

Foliage The leaves of a plant.

Food chain The relationship between living things that shows who gets eaten by whom.

Fronds The leaves of ferns.

Germination The growth of a seed when it starts to become a new plant.

Glucose A type of sugar produced by plants during photosynthesis.

Gymnosperm A type of plant, such as a conifer, which produces seeds that are not protected inside fruits.

Minerals Simple chemical substances that living things need to stay healthy. Plants get their minerals from the soil.

Nectar A sweet, energy-rich substance produced by many flowering plants to attract insects and other animals.

Ovary Part of the carpel where the ovules are and where seeds form.

Ovule Part of the ovary inside a carpel that develops into a seed after fertilization.

Parasite An organism that lives in or on another living thing, taking nourishment from it and causing it harm.

Petiole The stalk that joins a leaf to the stem of a plant.

Phloem Tubes that carry minerals and sugar from one part of the plant to another.

Photosynthesis The process by which plants make sugar from sunlight energy, carbon dioxide, and water.

Pollen Tiny grains produced in the male anthers of flowers; pollen must be carried to a stigma for pollination to take place.

Pollination The transfer of pollen from the male anther to the female stigma. Most flowers are pollinated by insects or the wind.

Pores Tiny openings in the surfaces of leaves that let air in and moisture out.

Radicle The first root to grow from a seed when it germinates.

Runner A slender stem that grows from the base of a plant to produce new plants.

Sepals Parts of a flower that protect the bud before it opens.

Spores The seeds of plants such as ferns and mosses; a spore grows into a new plant if conditions are right.

Stamen The male part of a flower that is made up of an anther on a long filament.

Starch A substance plants produce from the sugar they make during photosynthesis; starch can be stored in roots, seeds, and fruit as a source of energy.

Stem The part of a plant that connects its roots to its leaves and flowers; it carries water and food between the different parts.

Stigma The sticky top of the female carpel that captures the pollen grains.

Xylem Tubes that carry water to the different parts of a plant.

Web sites

www.kidsgardening.com/growingideas/projects/jan03/pg1.html
Ideas for creating a pollinator garden to bring flowers and insects together.

http://photoscience.la.asu.edu/photosyn/education/learn.html#amazing
What is photosynthesis? An Arizona State University site with links to many articles on photosynthesis.

http://www.urbanext.uiuc.edu/gpe/
This fun site from a University of Illinois Extension program features "The Great Plant Escape," a series of "mystery cases" that explore the world of plants and flowers.

http://waynesword.palomar.edu/trmar98.htm
A colorful introduction to the world of flowering plants.

Index

bamboo 11
beech 11
beetroot 9
berries 25
bluebonnet 4
buds 10, 11, 21, 27
bulbs 11
burdock 25

cabbage 10
cactus 11, 16, 17
carpels 20, 21
carrot 9
castor oil plant 19
catkin 21
cedar 7
celery 12
chlorophyll 17
coconuts 25
conifer 7
cucumber 24

daisy 21
dandelion 5, 21, 24
defenses 18–19
dog rose 19
duckweed 4, 5

eucalyptus 4, 5

ferns 7
fig 9
flowers 10, 20–21
food chain 14
fronds 7

fruits 10, 14, 24–25

germination 26–27
giant redwood 7
giant sequoia 7
grasses 4, 12, 18, 22

habitats 29
hawthorn 19
hornwort 6

insects 17, 19, 23
iris 10
ivy 16

leaves 5, 7, 10, 11, 12–13, 14–15, 16, 17, 27
liverwort 6
lotus plant 27

maple 24, 27
mosses 6

oak 4, 22, 27
onion 11
orchid 5, 24, 25

palm tree 13
parsley 4
pea 16, 24
petals 20, 21
photosynthesis 14, 15, 27, 29
pines 7, 9
poinsettia 21
pollen 21, 22, 23

pollination 22–23
pollution 29
poppy 28
potato 4, 11
prickles 19
pygmy weed 13

rainforests 7, 14, 17
roots 5, 7, 8, 9, 18, 26

seeds 7, 8, 20, 21, 23, 24–25, 26, 27, 28
sepals 20, 21
shoots 26, 27
soldier bug 19
spines 11, 17, 19
spores 6
stalks 6
stamens 20, 21
stems 5, 7, 10, 11, 17, 19, 27
stinking corpse lily 20
strawberry 10
succulents 16, 17
sunflower 21
sunlight 14, 15
sycamore 25

tendrils 16
thorns 11, 19
tubers 11

Venus flytrap 17

water lily 12, 17